AF598881

PAUL MOGENSEN

STEVEN PARRINO

PM / SP

Bob Nickas

Two very different artists, of different generations, one living and one not (the artist who was and will always be younger), artists whose work may have as much overlay as divergence, and who, though they never met, are brought into contact now by way of this exhibition, which neither of them will see.[1] Paul Mogensen, born 1941, Los Angeles; Steven Parrino, born 1958, New York, died New Year's Day 2005.

Mogensen's work from the mid-'60s to the early '70s was associated with Minimalism, included in exhibitions such as *A Romantic Minimalism*, *Structural Art*, *Cool Art*, and *Modular Painting*, shown alongside that of artists such as Carl Andre, Brice Marden, Robert Mangold, Agnes Martin, and David Novros. The designation Minimal Art, as befits the naming of a certain distillation, we can now imagine as a big box into which all sorts of art was placed, some because critics and curators didn't otherwise know what to do with it, while the original designation, as Mogensen has remarked, arose from one critic's dismissive attitude.[2] This certainly applies to other movements, at least in past periods when art was actually in motion. (Futurism, for example, and a time when artists looked ahead, when things, not only artworks, were being invented, as opposed to where we find ourselves today, in an ongoing, perhaps endless present.) Parrino's work, which first appeared in the '80s, is seen in relation to punk, conceptual pop, and the monochrome, shown in exhibitions with titles as direct as *Red* and *la couleur seule: l'experience du monochrome*, as clever as *Infotainment*, as preposterous as *Still Life With Transaction*. Among the range of artists with whom he often exhibited: John Armleder, Peter Halley, Jutta Koether, Olivier Mosset, and Cady Noland. With the exceptions of Neo-Expressionism—which made no sense to Parrino, as its "sound and fury" did not in any way reflect how the world felt to him, both on the surface and under the skin—and Neo-Geo, the '80s was a time of smaller boxes, expediently stacked, into which artists were imperfectly fit. We understand this period, which is also true of the '60s, as a time of disrupted narratives. An early exhibition in which Parrino would participate, *The Anticipated Ruin*, hints at the rhetorical mapping of the postmodern landscape that was undertaken in that moment. One of the few artists who made paintings neither abstract nor engaged with pictures, Parrino's key contribution was to physically interrupt the monochrome, the purity of its surface, as it had come down to him from Minimalism, and from which there was nothing remotely "romantic." In terms of human presence, his signature mis-stretched canvases—painting as unmade bed—only offer *dis-figuration*.

"I never think about the viewer. I think about what I want to do and then I do it. Then I don't look at it and it's just done."[3] Which of these artists said this? We can easily suppose it being either one of them. But it was Mogensen, a statement not dating to the mid-'60s, but from just a month ago. *"Do these paintings become models of a projected reasoning?"* Which of the two posed this question? Again, it might have been either, although you've probably already "reasoned" that it was Parrino.[4] It's clear that for both artists there is a certain indifference based on their belief in the work itself, as conceived, executed, and done. Their curious sense of detachment is, you might say, closely held. I knew Parrino well. Paul Mogensen and I have only recently met, so whatever I put forth in terms of his position and the products of his mind is my own view, from the outside looking in. And isn't this all criticism? A sort of ventriloquism? (Setting aside, of course, those critics and curators who are somehow clairvoyant.) Yet knowing one artist I am able to see the other in terms of those overlays, among them: No sign of the hand in the application of paint. No mixing of paint. Engaging with the wall and negative space. Composing with absence, a hole to perforate the

surface of a painting, cuts to disrupt the picture plane or its edge. Creating a sense of turning within the work, a circular motion that gives a still image its "live" experience—the "radiating line" works and spirals by Mogensen, begun in '65; Parrino's *Spin-Out Vortex*, 2000, and *Void Vortex*, 1996, to name just two works exploring this form, as well as his close connection to Robert Smithson's *Spiral Jetty*. There are distinctions, of course. The hard color / hard form affirmed by Mogensen in an early statement by Carl Andre[5] stands in contrast to Parrino's perverse play of hard color / soft form. In parallel, Mogensen and Parrino have both engaged metallic color, high gloss to reflect light, spray paint, industrial material, painting as installation. Mogensen's 11-panel work, exhibited in 1978, in a specially built room, a single work of and hung in progression around all four walls, is experiential, time-based, unable to be apprehended, neither by camera nor the human eye in an instant. Parrino's *13 Shattered Panels (for Joey Ramone)*, 2001, a destroyed room comprised of 13 black elements, is clearly not canvas on traditional support, but boards splintered and damaged, the sign of the hand—the entire body—after the brush has been set aside, re-action painting, an amplification of gestural painting, silence and noise. Neither artist had the slightest fear of emptiness, which Mogensen identifies as *horror vacui*, a term Parrino would no doubt immensely enjoy.

Mogensen came to art after studying math and chemistry, on a scholarship thanks to Southern California's aerospace industry, the progressions of his paintings based on mathematics, which he distinguishes from an art of numbers and counting. (Here we are reminded of the conceptual artist Hanne Darboven in the '60s, and the painter Xylor Jane today, an artist with numbers tattooed on all her fingers, the digits with which we first learn to count.) Color is central to Mogensen's work, his paintings are based on the periodic table. It's important to note that this is an artist who is interested in geometry, not in math, but uses it to realize his work, while the actual math, rather than written down and determined, exists "in his head."[6] In Mel Bochner's 1967 essay, "Serial Art, Systems, Solipsism," Mogensen's art is associated with the serial methodology of Jo Baer, Darboven, Dan Graham, Sol LeWitt, Smithson, as well as the photography of Edweard Muybridge, and his own work. Bochner writes:

Seriality is premised on the idea that the succession of terms (divisions) within a single work is based on a numerical or otherwise predetermined deviation (progression, permutation, rotation, reversal) from one or more of the preceding terms in that piece. Furthermore the idea is carried out to its logical conclusion, which, without adjustments based on taste or chance, is the work. No stylistic or material qualities unite the artists using this approach because what form the work takes is unimportant (some of these artists have ceased to make "things.")[7]

Recently in Mogensen's studio, referring to his work, he said something which suddenly sucked the air out of the room: *"I don't care what it looks like."*[8] Catching my breath, I reacted with the sort of surprise that will eventually evaporate. Even though this was a first meeting, the artist came across as someone forthright and direct in speaking about what he does, and doesn't do, someone who would never say anything simply for effect. In this I was reminded of Parrino, and of how he, in a certain circumstance, might have said the very same thing: *"I don't care what it looks like."* This is a startling admission on the face of it. And yet, thinking back to Bochner, you understand that as a plain-spoken expression of the attitude behind the work—distinct from its surface and surface effects—it's true. What form the work takes may be important to us, may even seduce us, but this is not necessarily of primary interest to the person who brought it into the world, and once here it has a life of its own. It will be shown, written about, for better or for worse, it may be bought and sold, it may disappear and re-emerge. All this occurs outside the studio, beyond the artist, beyond their intentions and activity, often well after-the-fact, and if we are drawn to these works—and we are, clearly—the artist might think but never say: That's your problem. And it's not a bad problem to have, for collectors, critics, curators, the gallery- and museum-going public, never larger than ever before, which may know little about art, math, geometry, color theory, esthetics, and it won't matter.

When Mogensen spoke these words, I was standing next a recent work, set slightly raised off the floor, a lustrous pink and alizarin crimson painting, still wet (and likely always seeming so), that reminded me of the same color combination, though in Mogensen's work of heightened gloss, in now-classic paintings by Mary Heilmann—*Pink Knot*, *Save the Last Dance For Me*, both 1979. Here, I thought also of how, with only rare exception, Mogensen does not title his works. (Are there more than three? I can name *Copperopolis*, *Black Widow*, and *Stealth*, no others, and the artist would insist these have little to do with the actual works before us.) Mogensen, whose ongoing approach eliminates any decision-making deemed unnecessary, also dismisses the notion of titles as "ways into" a work, clues to meaning, ways of reading, and so on. In this he differs significantly from Parrino, for whom titles were an actively engaged part of his project, but then he was also on numerous occasions publishing short texts, and there is no writer divorced from titles entirely. With Mogensen what we have, and not for reading into but for seeing, is color:

Ultramarine Blue, Prussian Blue, Cobalt Blue, Thalo Blue, Persian Red, Earth Red, Cadmium Red, Cadmium Yellow, Cadmium Orange, Vine Black, Ivory Black, Portland Gray, Alizarin Crimson, Manganese Violet, Titanium White.

He has confessed to opening the caps on tubes of paint in art supply stores, despite the prohibition, to see what the color actually looks like, not trusting the name on the label, or the color's diffused appearance in its container. As for titles, both Mogensen and Parrino might agree, they serve merely as the names of things—a painting in name only. Color is what painting is made from.

The pairing of artists is sometimes predictable, and sometimes takes us by surprise. Such is the case with this modest presentation of works by Mogensen and Parrino. A more expansive show in future, with the point of entry established, would be something worth looking forward to.

Notes

1. When asked if he would go to Brussels for the show, Mogensen seemed casually unconcerned about the need to do so. And further, when asked if he had seen the work of Parrino, even in reproduction, he said that he had not. The author in conversation with Paul Mogensen, studio visit, New York, Aug. 20, 2018.

2. In an interview with Hans Ulrich Obrist, conducted in the studio, July 2018, for a book to be published by Karma, New York. Mogensen, when asked about the term Minimal art, recalled being at Yale in 1962, where minimal art was never discussed, and commented: "... that name hadn't been coined. Barbara Rose saw some of this work years later and she was Frank Stella's wife. He didn't like it and she hated it, so she called it minimal. That's why it was called that. There is a tradition of attacks by critics naming art movements." Transcript page 3.

3. Ibid, Obrist conversation, transcript page 12.

4. Steven Parrino, text published in *Perverted By Language*, Hillwood Art Gallery, Long Island University, 1987, page 54.

5. Carl Andre, "New In New York: Line Work," *Arts Magazine*, May 1967.

6. Studio visit, New York, Aug. 20, 2018.

7. Mel Bochner, "Serial Art, Systems, Solipsism," *Arts Magazine*, Summer 1967.

8. Studio visit, New York, Aug. 20, 2018.

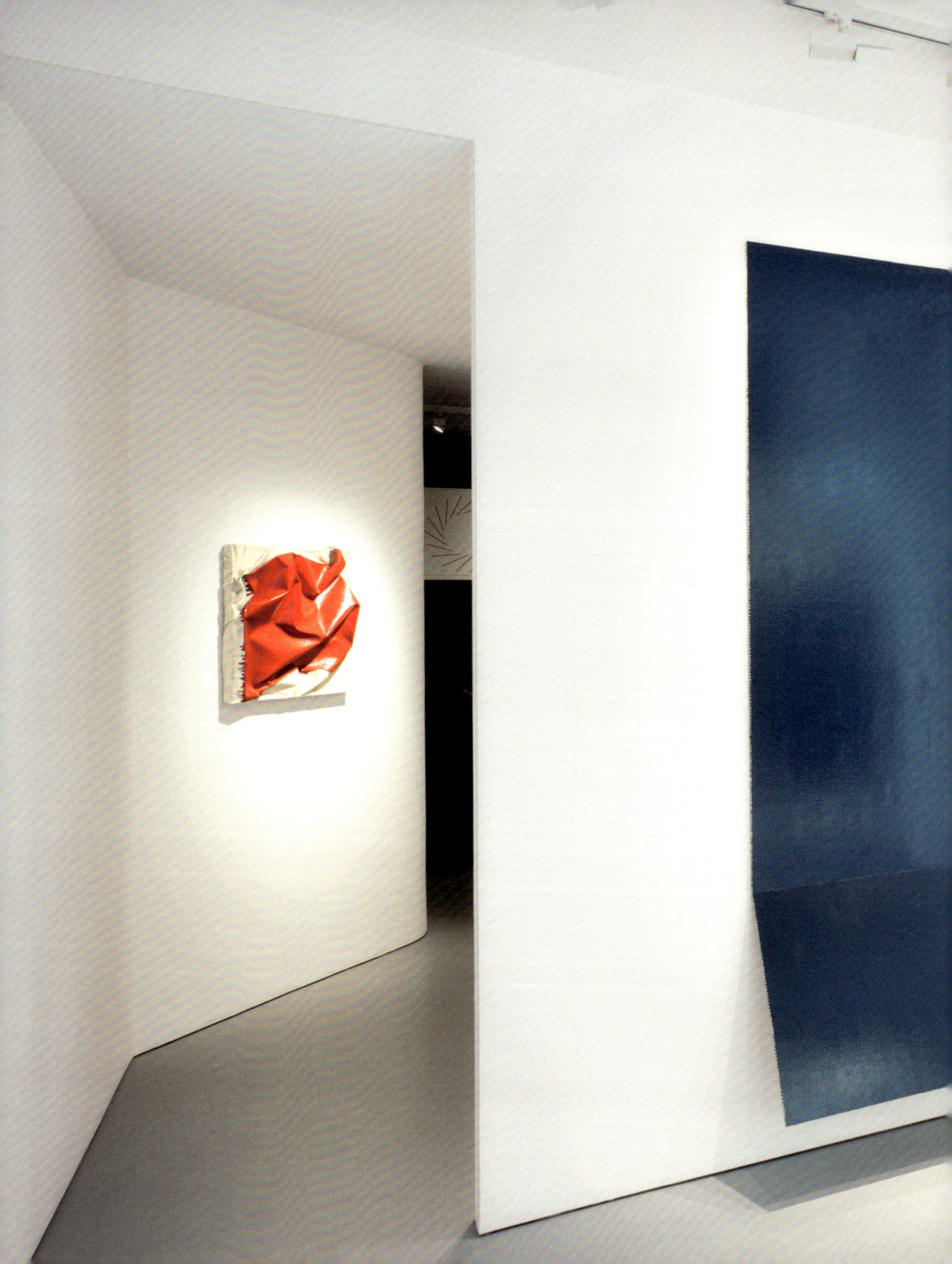

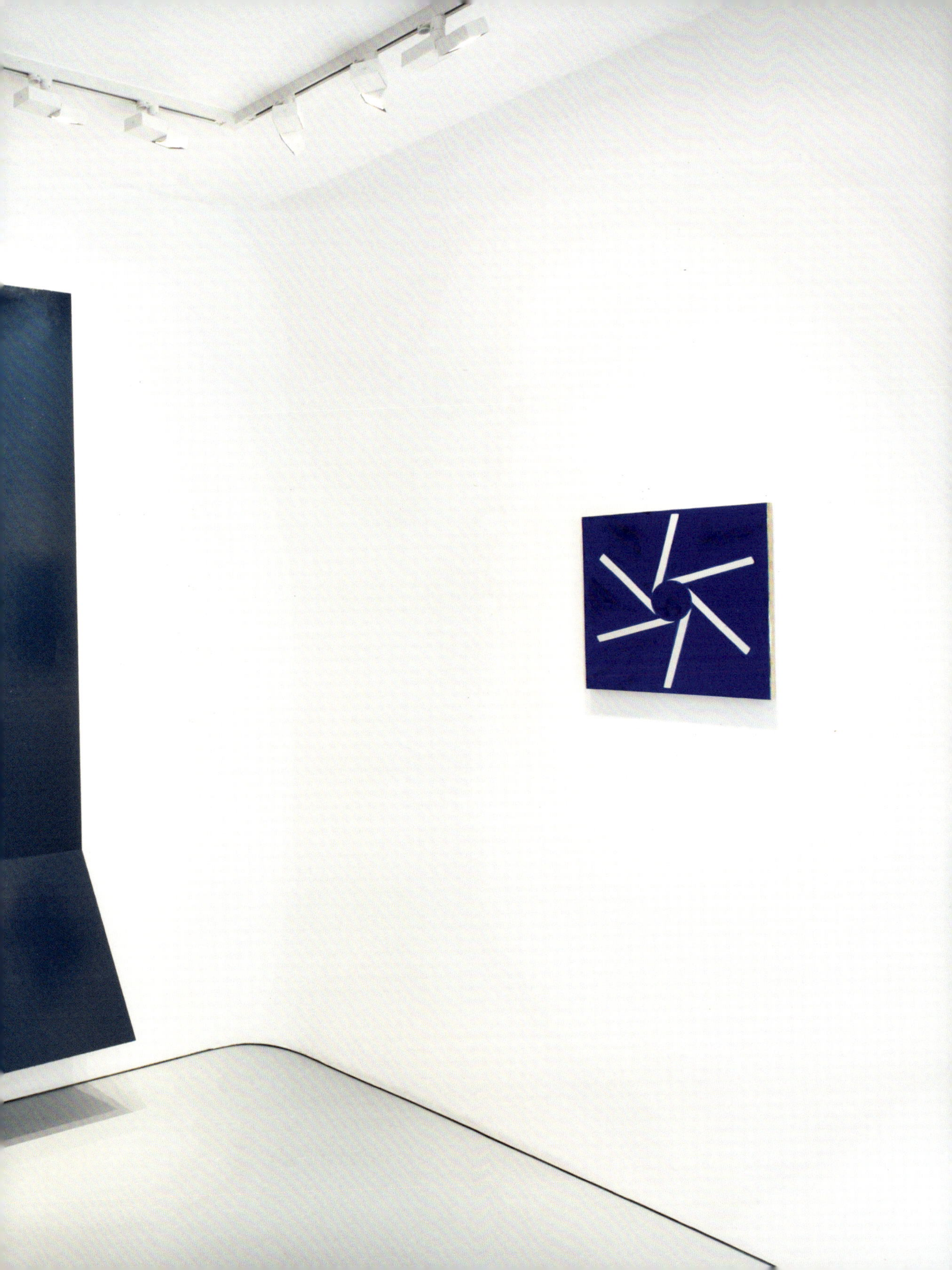

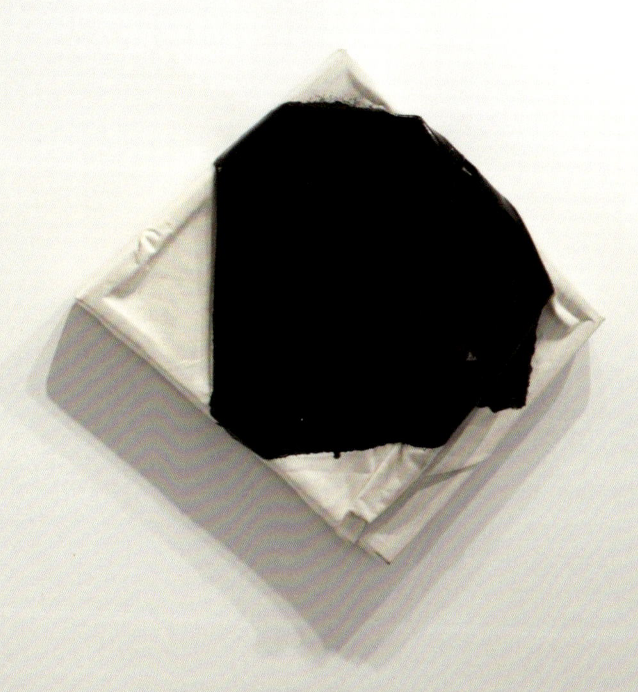

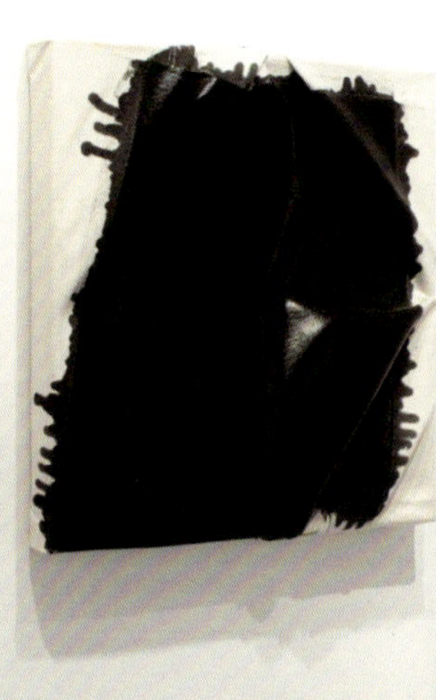

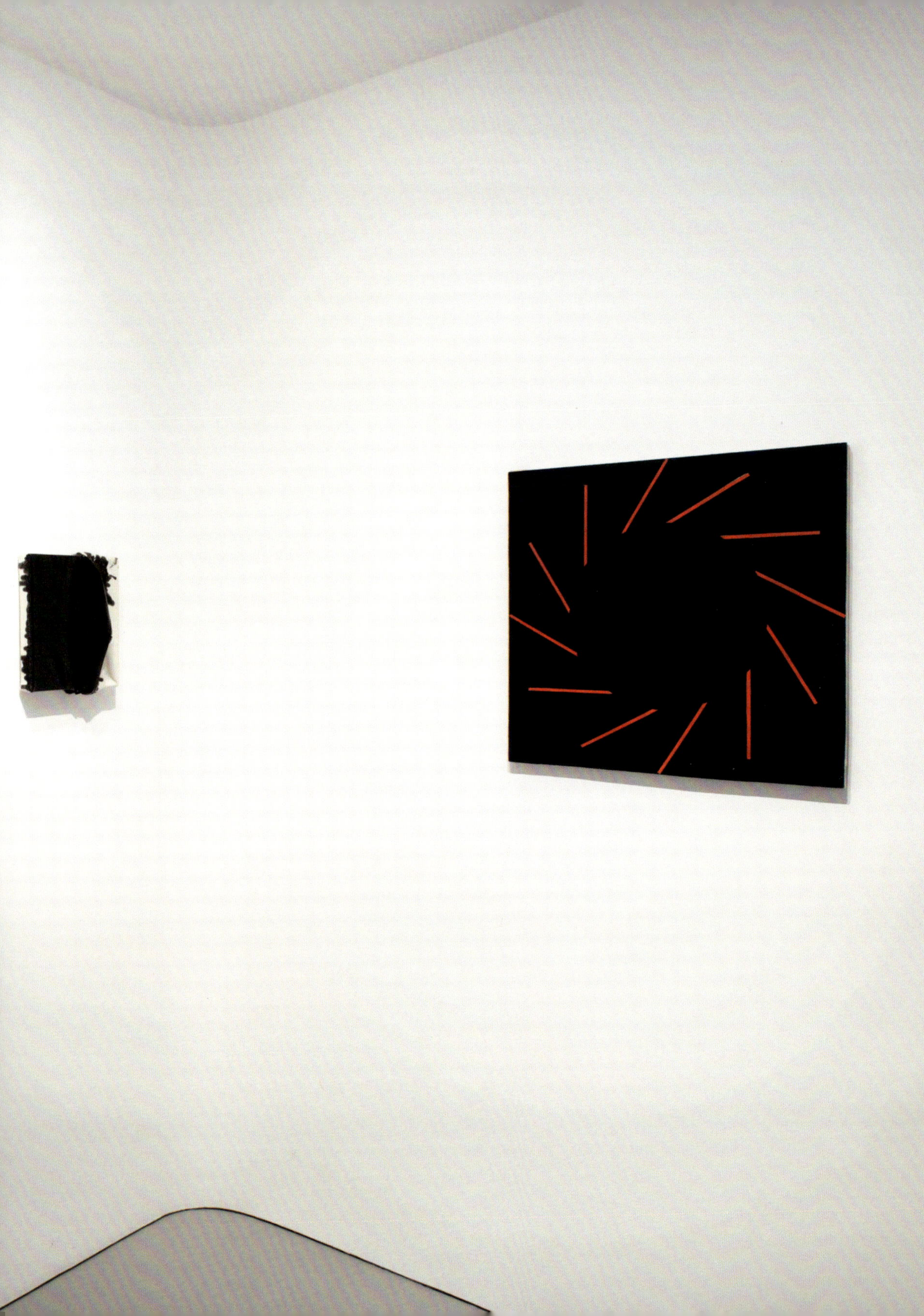

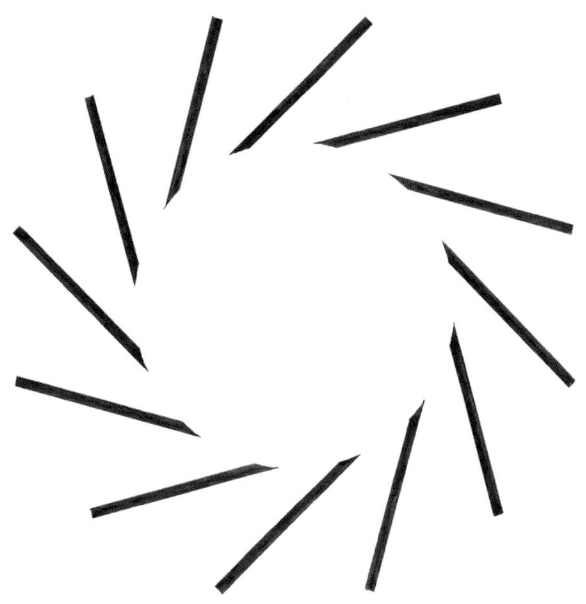

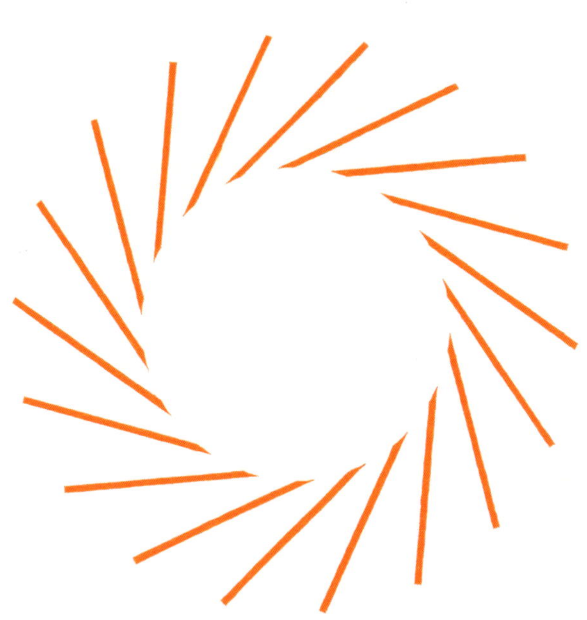

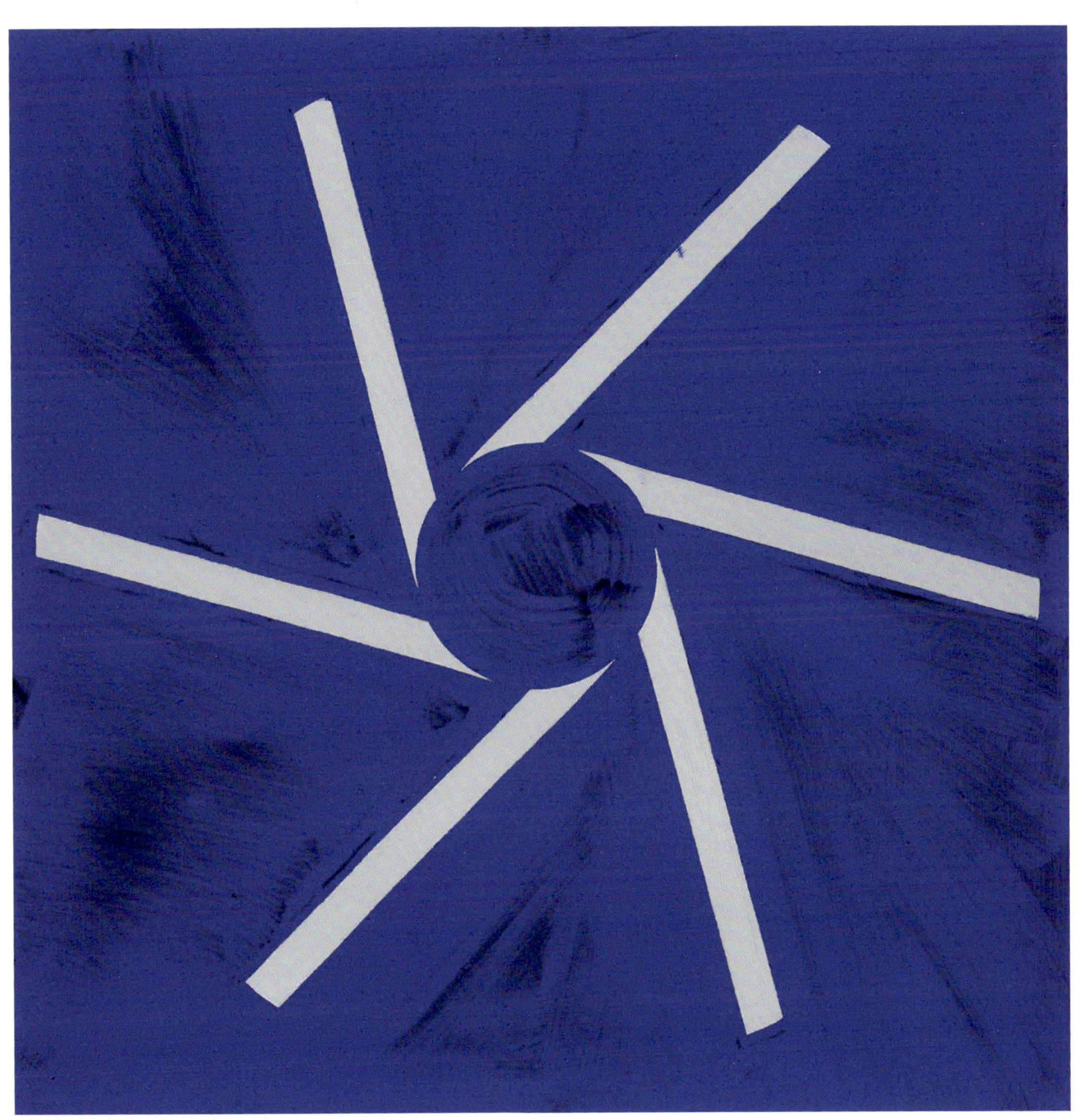

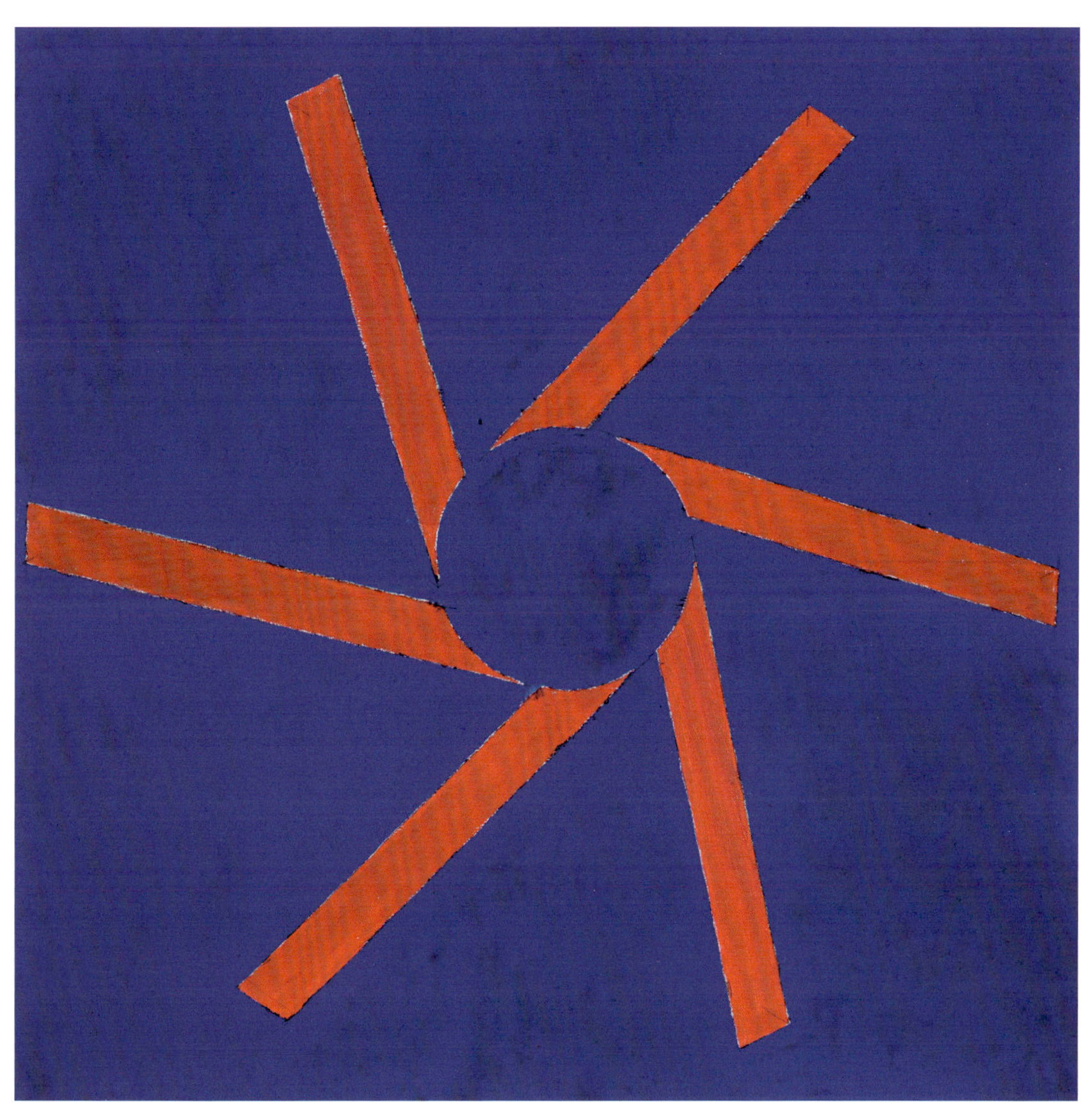

04

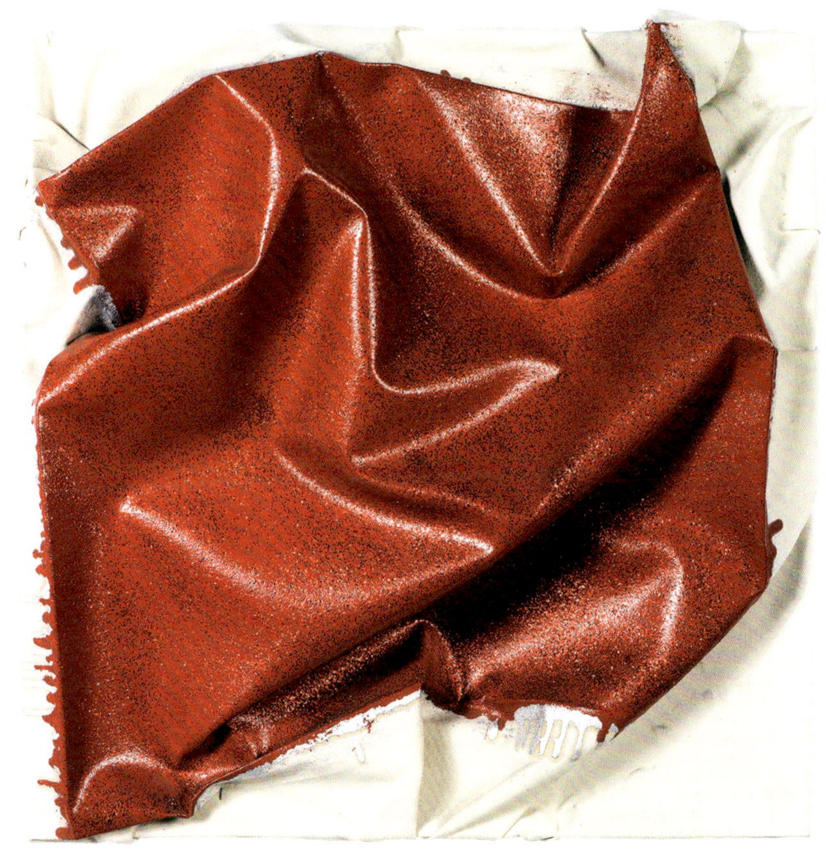

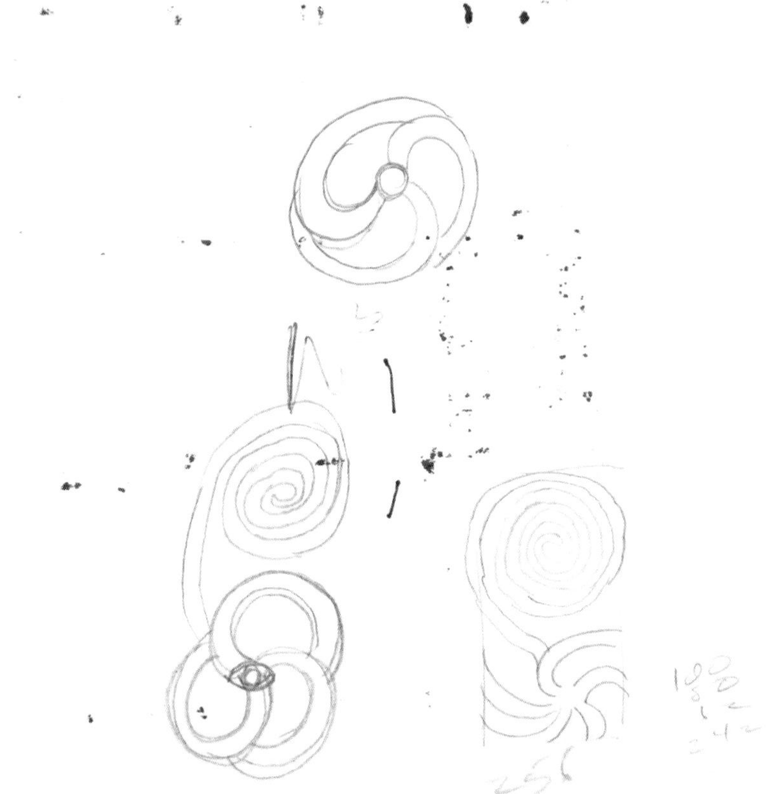

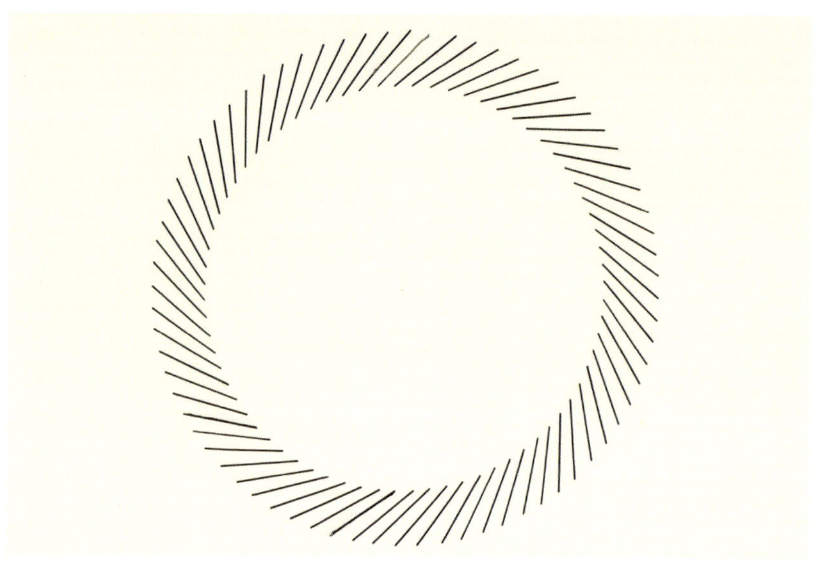

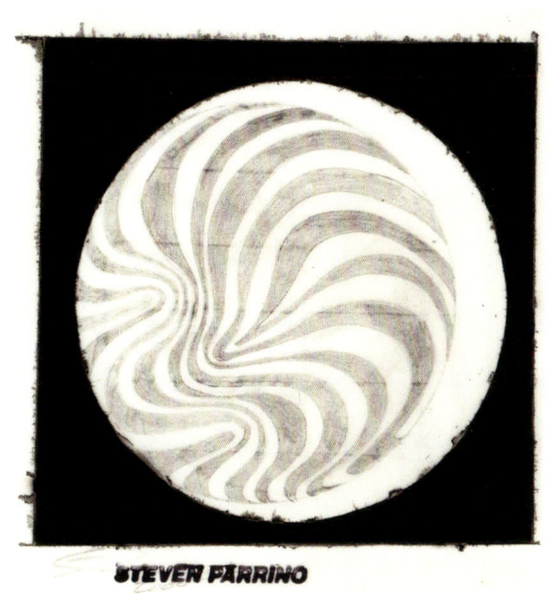
STEVEN PARRINO

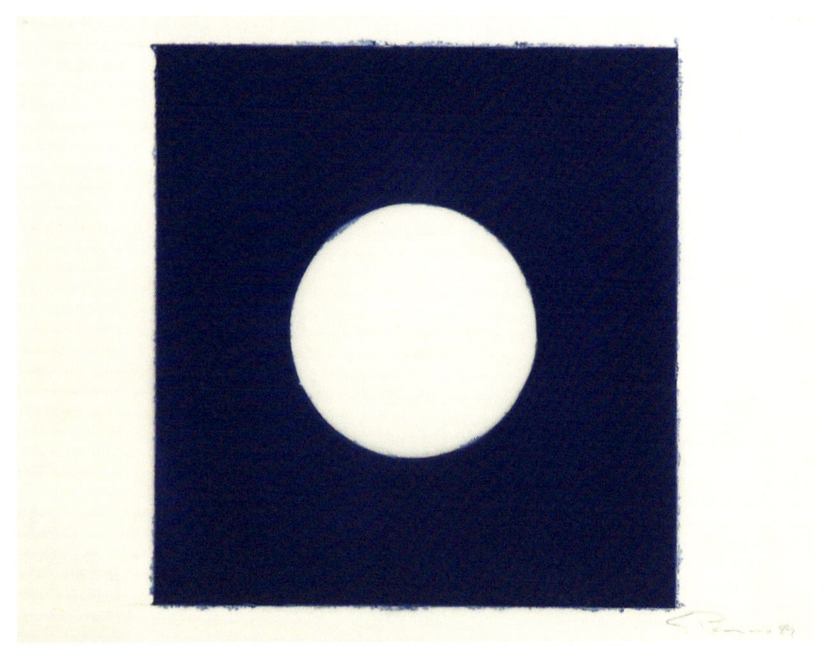

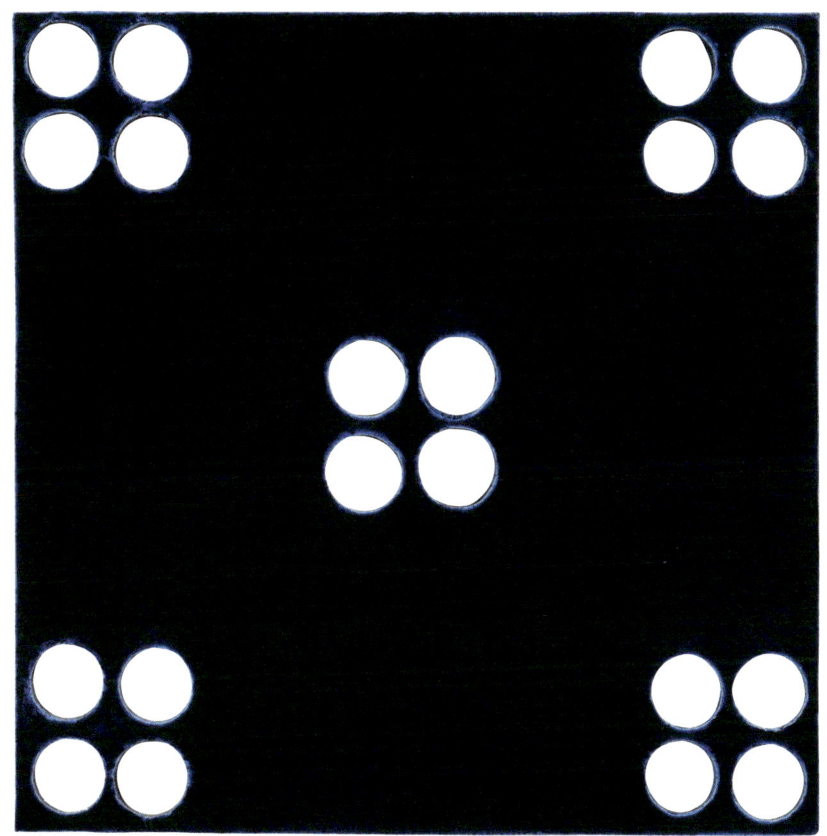

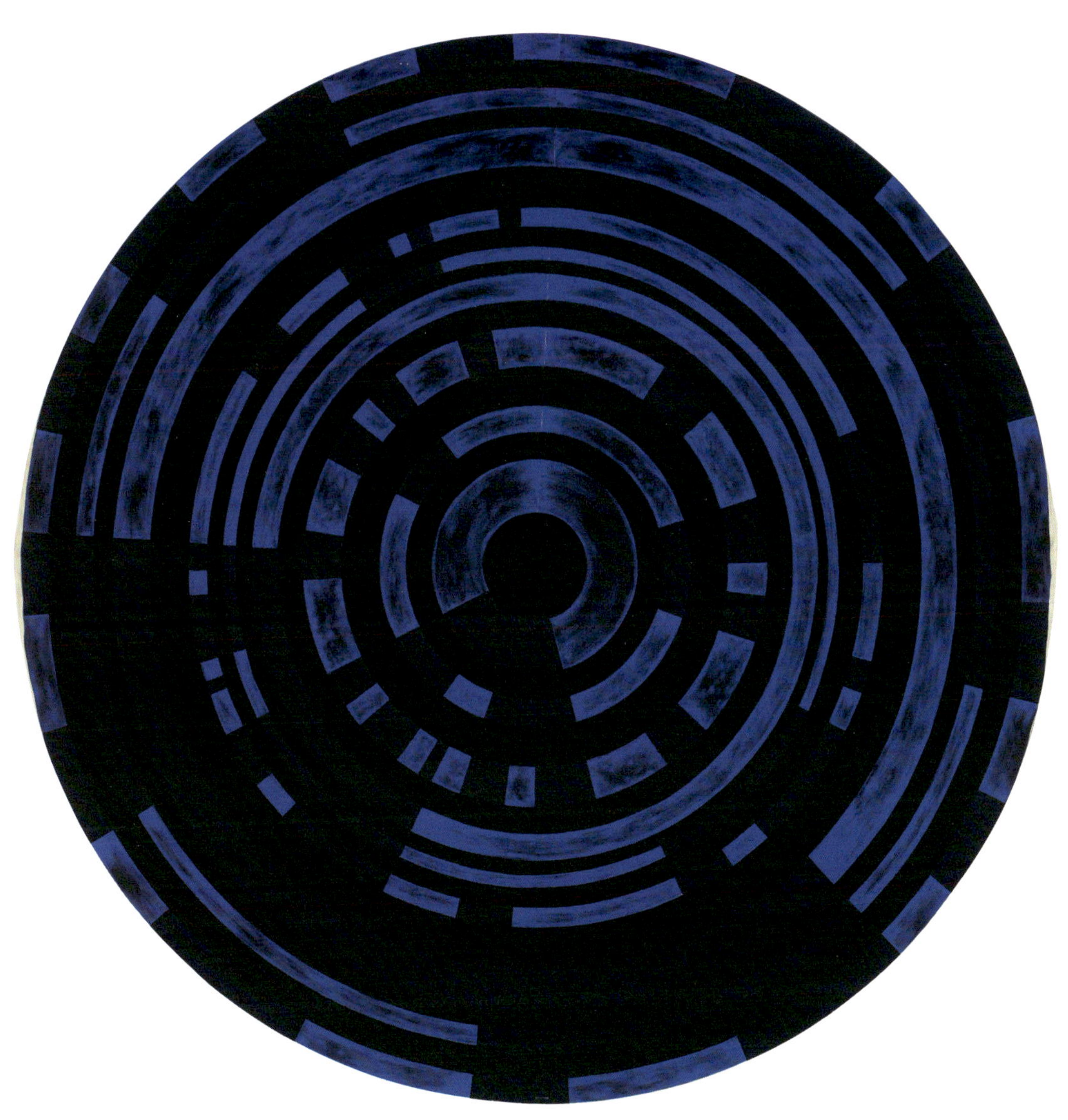

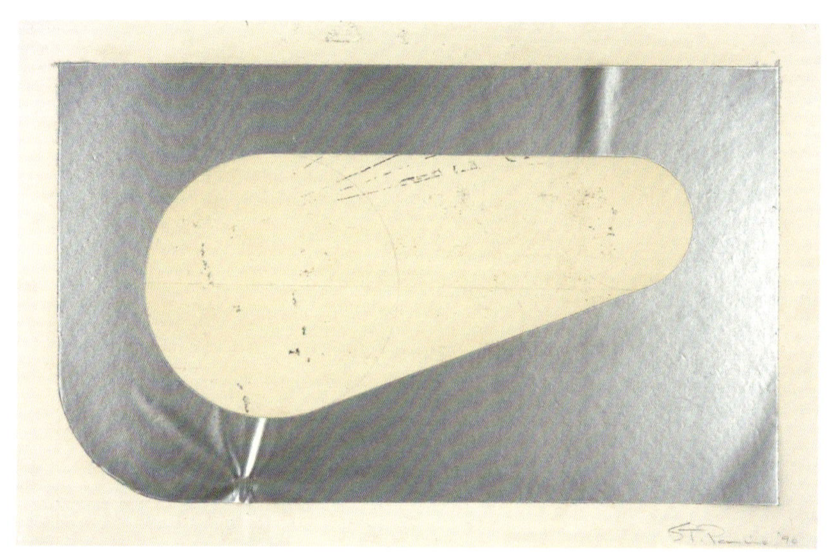

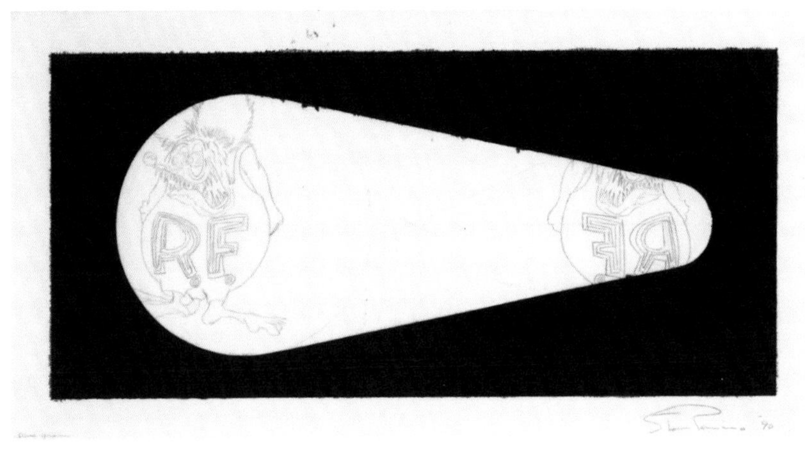
RF

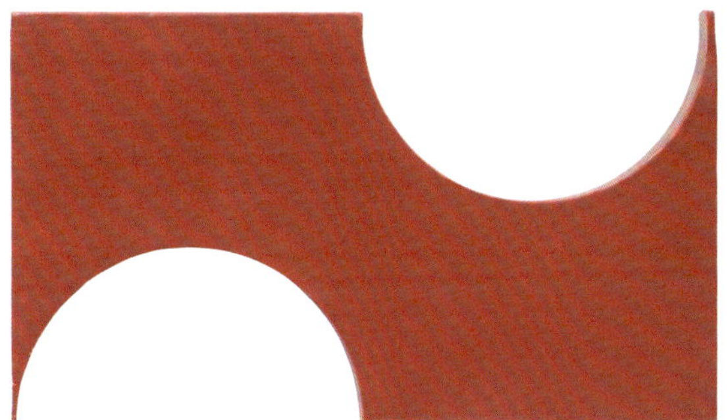

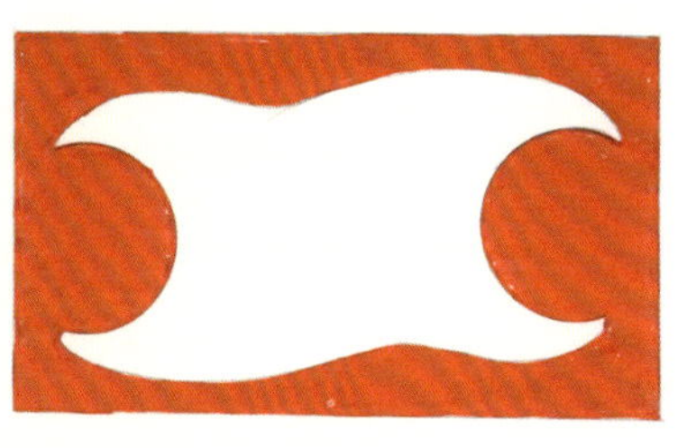

STEVEN PARRINO

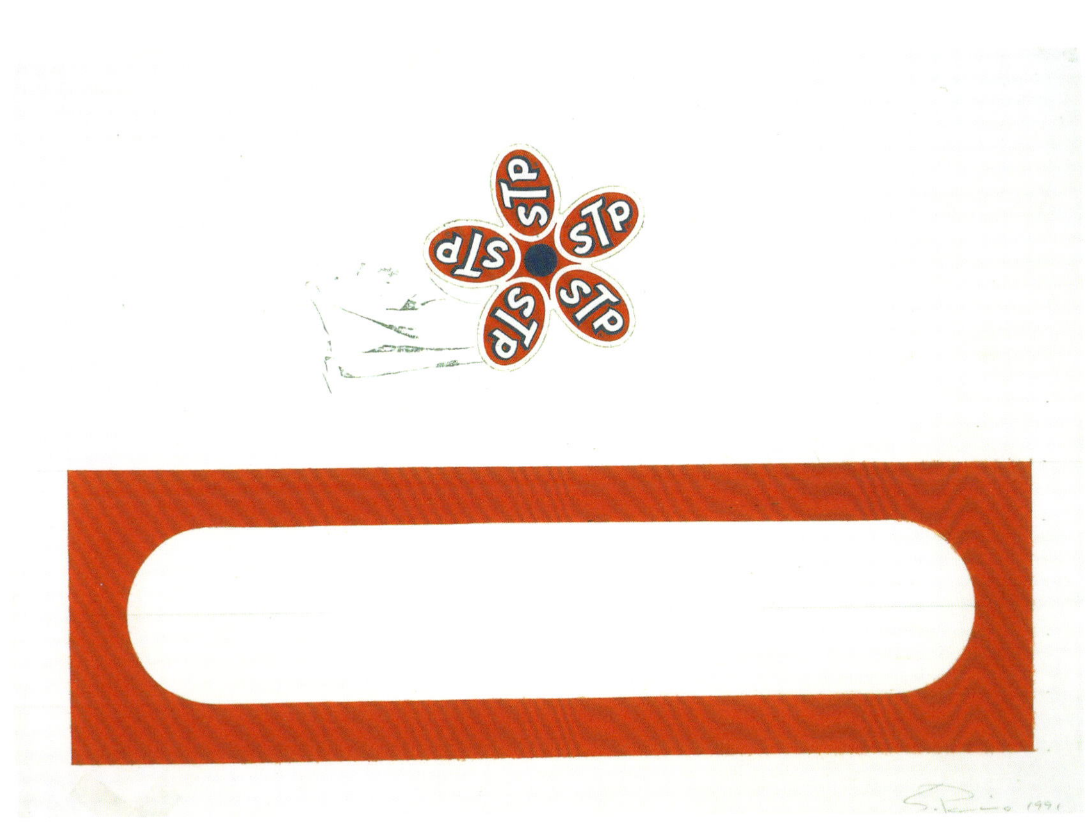
STP
STP
STP
STP
STP

STEVEN PARRINO

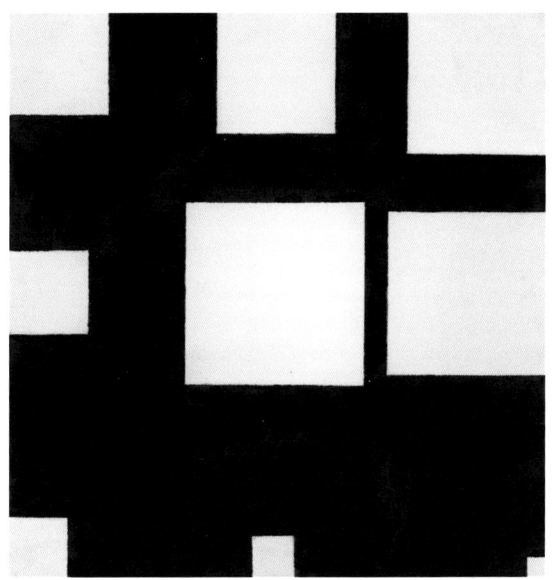

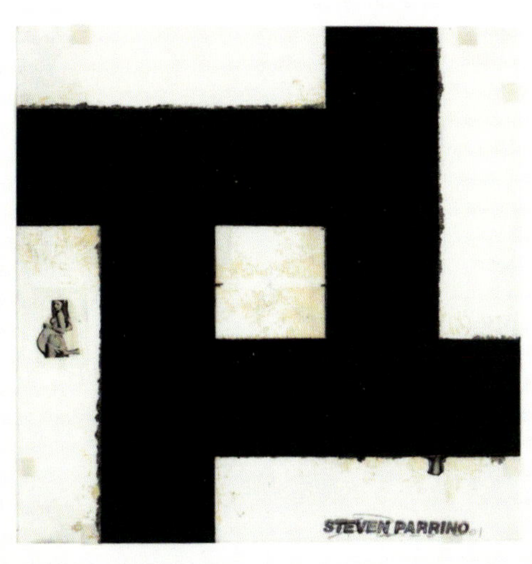
STEVEN PARRINO

JERK

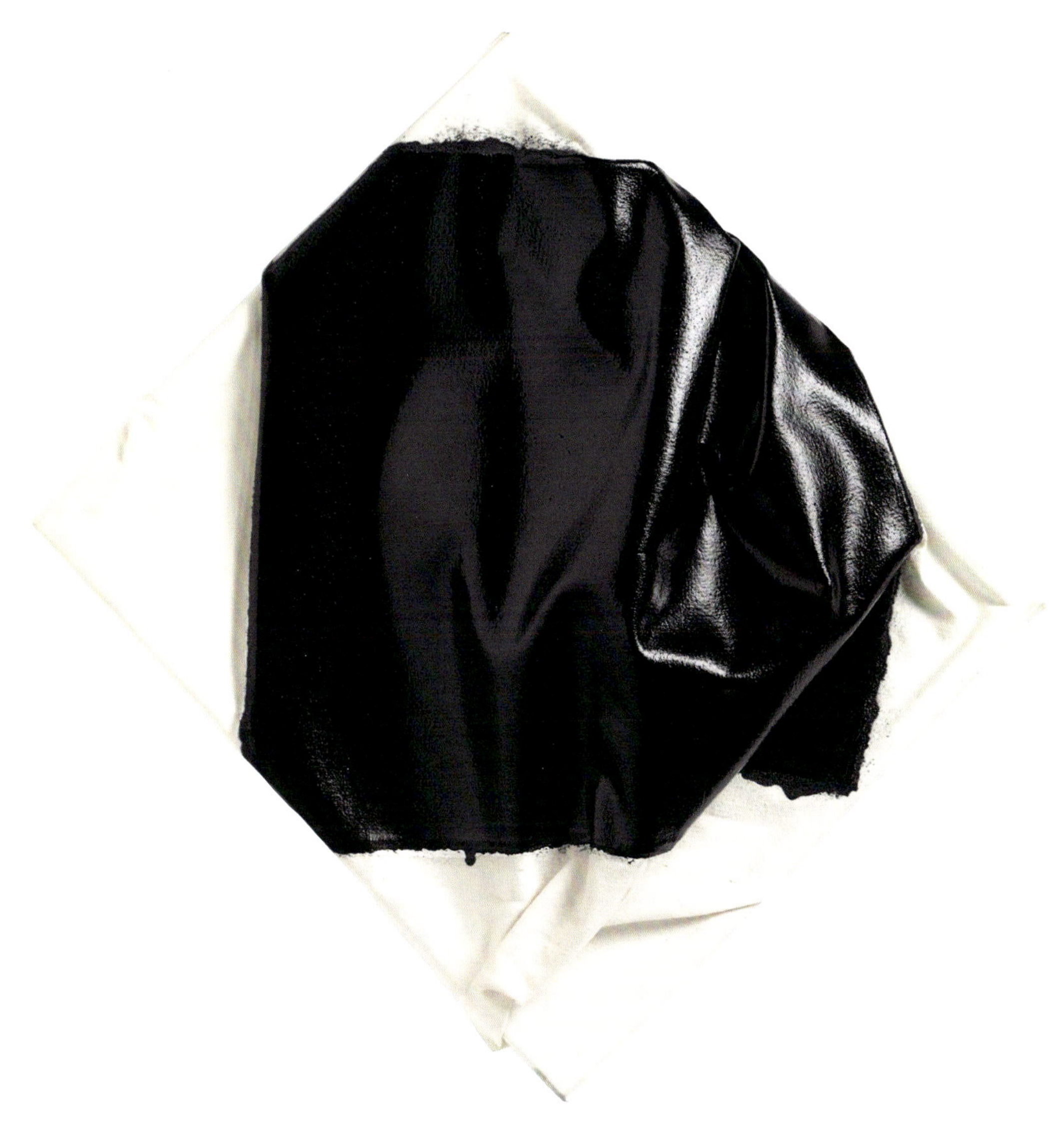

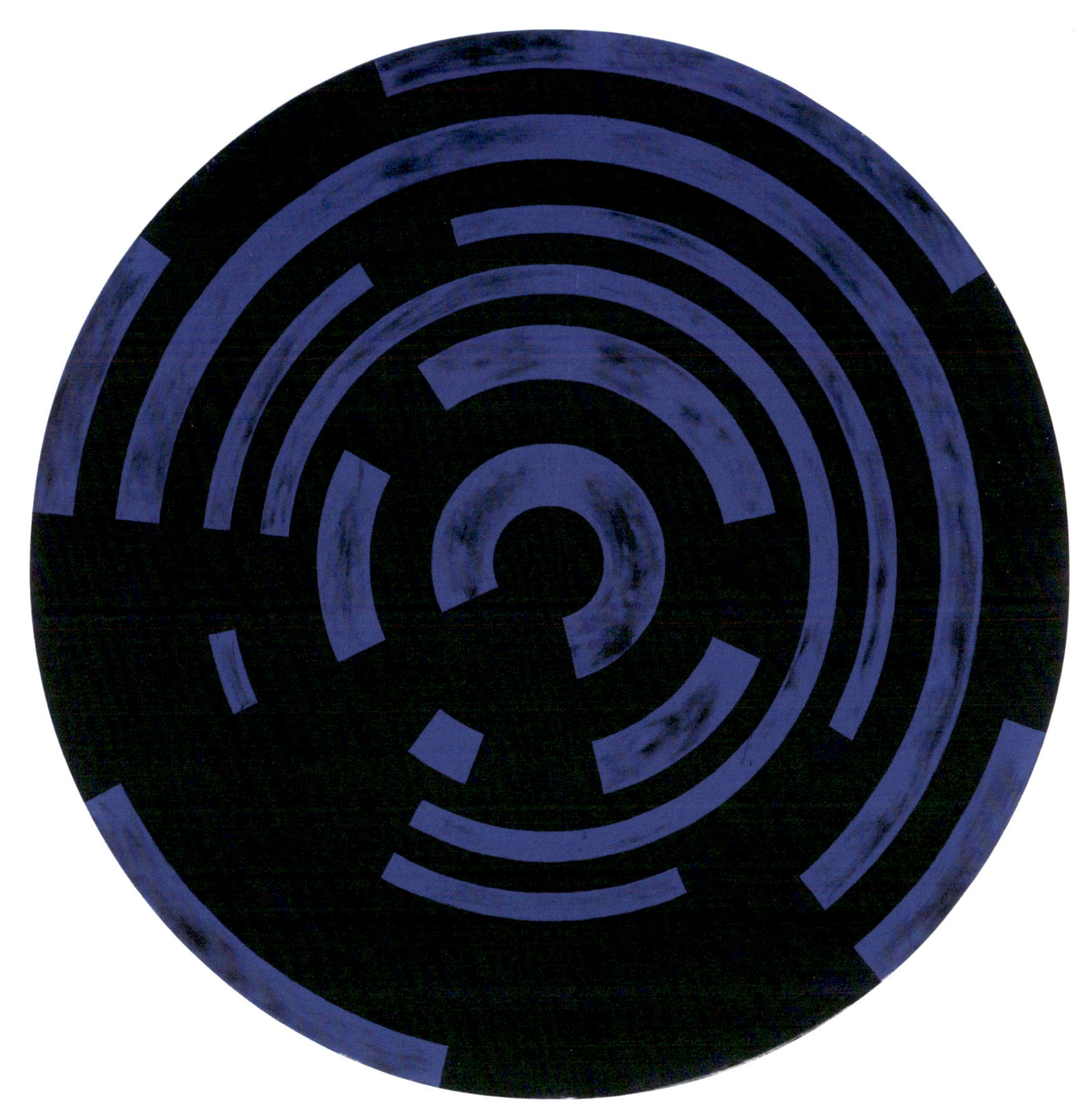

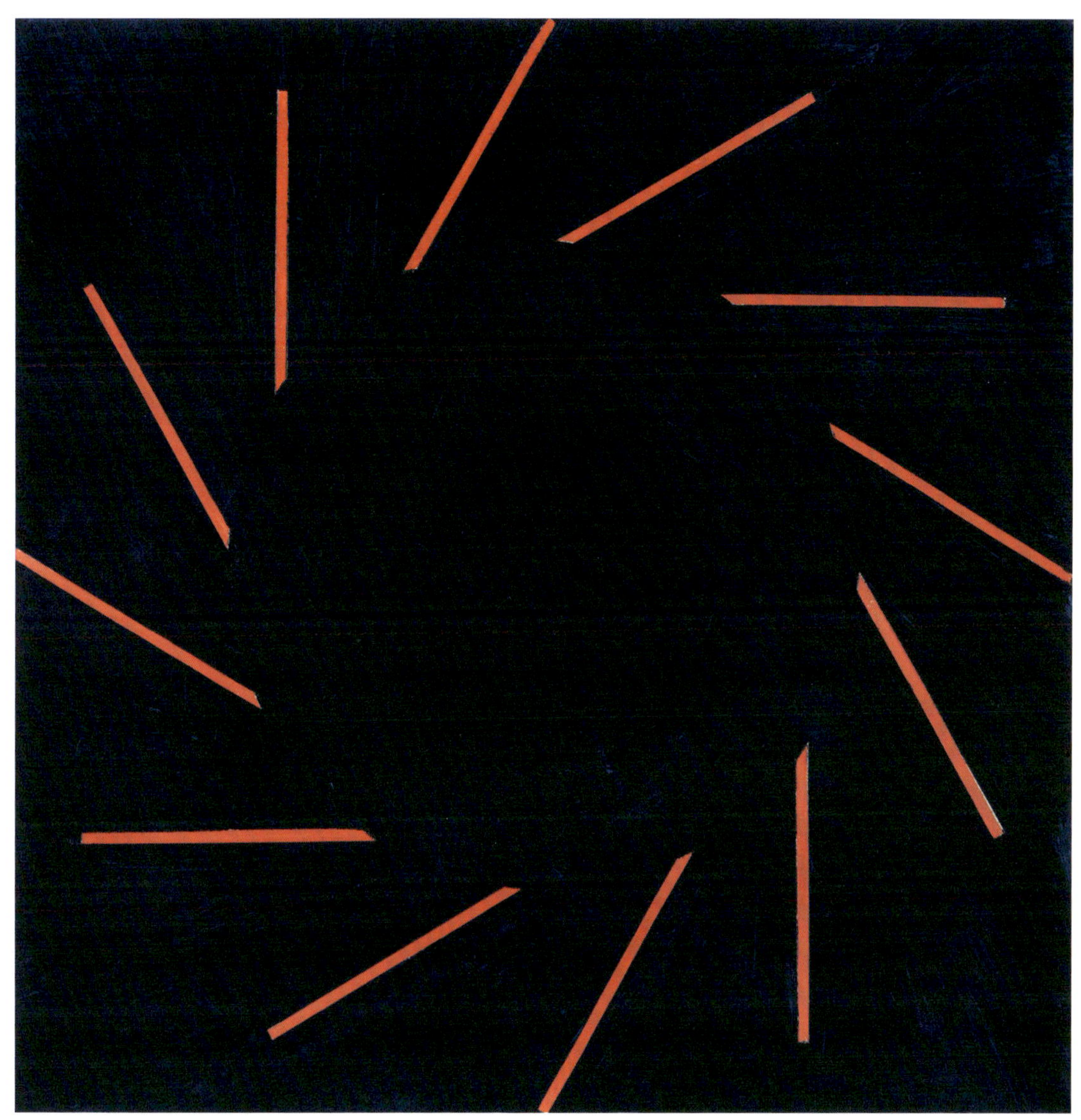

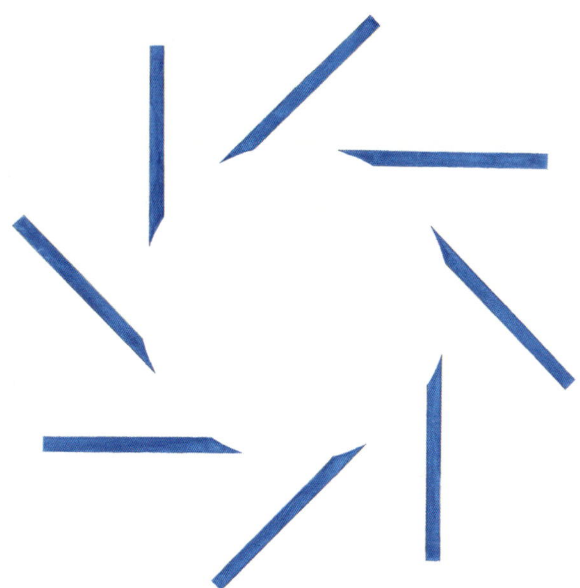

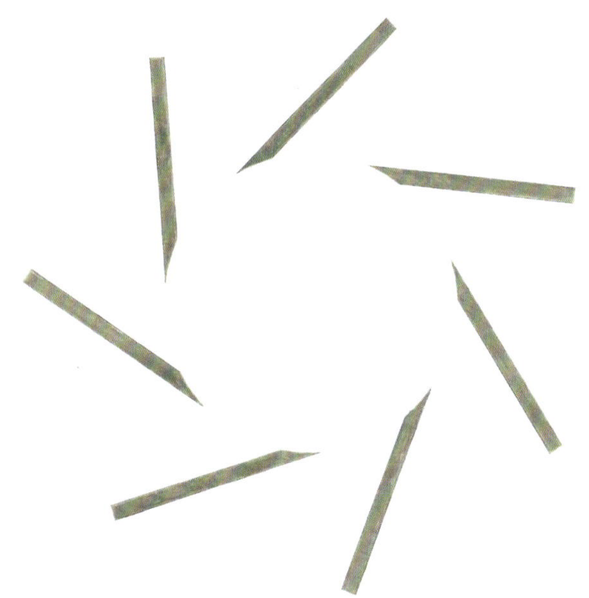

01
Paul Mogensen
no title, 2012
Watercolor and graphite on paper
22 ¼ × 30 inches (56.5 × 76 cm)

02
Paul Mogensen
no title, 2012
Acrylic on paper (cadmium orange)
22 ⅜ × 30 inches (57 × 76 cm)

03
Paul Mogensen
no title, 2016
Oil on canvas
18 × 18 inches (46 × 46 cm)

04
Paul Mogensen
no title (cadmium red and ultramarine blue), 2018
Oil on canvas
12 × 12 inches (30.5 × 30.5 cm)

05
Steven Parrino
Untitled, 1999
Enamel on canvas
24 7⁄16 × 24 inches (62 × 61 cm)

06
Paul Mogensen
no title (ivory black), 2017
Gloss acrylic and gouache on canvas
96 × 96 inches (243.8 × 243.8 cm)

07
Steven Parrino
Untitled (sketch), n.d.
Pen on paper
Overall dimensions variable

08
Paul mogensen
no title, 2002
Ink on paper
15 × 22 ¼ inches (38.1 × 56.5)

09
Steven Parrino
Untitled, 2000
Enamel and graphite on vellum
7 ⅞ × 7 inches (20 × 17.8 cm)

10
Paul mogensen
no title, 2012
Acrylic and gouache on paper
15 ¼ × 22 inches (38.7 × 55.9 cm)

11
Paul Mogensen
Untitled, 1989
Enamel on vellum
9 × 12 inches (22.9 × 30.5 cm)

12
Paul Mogensen
no title, 1997
Oil on canvas
36 × 36 inches (91.4 × 91.4 cm)

13
Paul Mogensen
no title (Stealth series), 1986
Oil on canvas
120 inches (304.8 cm) in diameter

14
Steven Parrino
Untitled, 1990
Graphite and enamel on vellum paper
11 ¾ × 19 inches (29.8 × 48.3 cm)

15
Steven Parrino
Untitled (Dan Graham), 1990
Enamel and graphite on vellum
9 ¾ × 18 ¾ inches (24.8 × 47.6 cm)

16
Paul Mogensen
no title, 1997
Enamel on MDF
4 ¾ × 8 ¼ inches (12.1 × 21 cm)

17
Steven Parrino
Untitled, 1987
Graphite and marker on vellum
9 × 12 inches (22.9 × 30.5 cm)

18
Steven Parrino
Untitled, 1991
Enamel, graphite, ink, and sticker on vellum paper
13 × 19 inches (33 × 48.3 cm)

19
Paul Mogensen
no title, 2012
Acrylic on paper (gloss cadmium red)
15 ¼ × 22 inches (39 × 56 cm)

20
Paul Mogensen
Standard, 1966
Oil on canvas
4 parts; 96 × 96 inches (243.8 × 243.8 cm) overall

21
Steven Parrino
Untitled, n.d.
Sprayed engine enamel on vellum
9 × 9 inches (22.9 × 22.9 cm)

22
Steven Parrino
Study for V.S., 2003
Enamel on canvas
12 × 12 inches (30.5 × 30.5 cm)

23
Paul Mogensen
no title, 2018
Acrylic and oil on Masonite panel
12 ¼ × 12 inches (31.1 30.5 cm)

24
Steven Parrino
Untitled, 2001
Sprayed enamel + newsprint collage
with clear tape on vellum
9 × 9 inches (22.9 × 22.9 cm)

25
Steven Parrino
Untitled, 1985
Enamel and graphite on vellum
14 × 11 inches (35.6 × 27.9 cm)

26
Paul Mogensen
no title, 2012
Acrylic and gouache on paper
15 ¼ × 22 1⁄16 inches (39 × 56 cm)

27
Steven Parrino
Untitled, 1995
Enamel on canvas
18 11⁄16 × 18 11⁄16 inches (45.7 × 45.7 cm)

28
Steven Parrino
Untitled, 1990
Enamel on honeycomb aluminum
93 ¾ × 48 × 11 ¾ inches (238.1 × 121.9 × 29.8 cm)

29
Steven Parrino
Misfit #4, 1995
Enamel and gesso on canvas
20 ⅞ × 20 ⅞ inches (53 × 53 cm)

30
Paul Mogensen
no title, 1986
Oil on canvas
96 inches (243.8 cm) in diameter

31
Paul Mogensen
no title, 2008
Oil on panel
24 × 24 inches (61 × 61 cm)

32
Paul Mogensen
no title, 2012
Watercolor on paper (cobalt blue)
22 ⅜ × 30 inches (57 × 76 cm)

33
Paul Mogensen
no title, 2012
Watercolor and graphite on paper (Davy's gray)
22 ⅛ × 30 inches (56 × 76 cm)

Paul Mogensen – Steven Parrino

Published on the occasion of the exhibition at

OV Project
Brussels, Belgium
September 6–October 20, 2018

Published by Karma Books, New York

Edition of 500

Special thanks to the Parrino Family Collection
and Gagosian Gallery

ISBN 978-1-949172-12-6